LIVE SIMPLY
LESS IS MORE!

by
Candess M. Campbell, PhD

Vesta Enterprises, Inc.
Spokane, (WA) 99201.
http://candesscampbell.com

Book Interior, Cover Design and E-book Design by Amit Dey |
amitdey2528@gmail.com

First printing: 2020

ISBN: 978-1-7351363-0-1

Live Simply: Less Is More *is written in a simplistic meditative style, and that is the perfect antidote for a world gone mad with technology and information that easily overwhelms the senses. The words are soothing and for anyone who chooses to do the exercises, there is no choice except to slow down and take stock of your life. The exercises are simple yet profound. They are as applicable for a child as for an adult. Ideally, parents will find themselves doing the exercises with their children.*

Pat Dougherty,
Holistic Chiropractor

As a Bibliophilic, who is committed to lowering my carbon footprint and simplifying my own life, I would recommend that **Live Simply: Less is More** *to be a part of your library. Candess is a quality therapist, healer, world traveler, and teacher and has spent thousands of hours with people. One chapter, one sentence stem in this book will change your life. This is practical, the rubber that meets the road stuff, yet it feels very spiritually satisfying: like eating a super nutritious meal where a small portion fills you up.*

Cheyenne Mendel,
Acupuncturist and Bazi Practitioner

Live Simply: Less is More *is a must-read for anyone who wants to experience more inner peace, less stress, and more effective boundaries. Candess addresses the implications that stress has in our lives and gives us a recipe for living our lives with more balance and flow. Candess provides writing prompts at the* end of each chapter to get clear about each topic and offers time for reflection. As someone who used to "Should" on myself and lacked effective personal boundaries, this book is an excellent addition to my personal development library."

Tandy Elisala,
Family Caregiver Coach and
Success Coach https://tandyelisala.com

Every chapter of **Live Simply: Less is More** *revitalized the notion within me that the soul needs more care than we often tend to give it and by doing so, we open up a world of peace, joy, and fulfillment that knocks overwhelm off its feet. Candess M. Campbell especially brings these principles into action with her Soul Stems and meditation techniques. A true must-read for the soul.*

Nacrissa J Vil,
Author of Gravitate: Activating the
8 Magnetic Relationship Strengths
To Attract The Love You Want

Table of Contents

Introduction

It's your life! With **Live Simply: Less is More**, you can regain your life, expand your time and space, and live the life you dream! This book was written as a self-prescription. Given that many of us teach what we need to learn, this book was a gentle and easy creation. What I loved about writing daily is that it permitted me to do what my heart and my soul truly wanted, which was to be able to continue the creative work I love and to do it without giving up my Self in the process.

Now, you too have the opportunity to live the life you desire while staying connected to yourSelf and your loved ones.

At the end of this book **Live Simply: Less is More**, you will find a list to recognize your stress symptoms. If you are really stressed, you may want to read through the book to help you to slow down, find peace, take more control of your creations, and become less stressed. There is an **Opportunity** at the end of each chapter, which is either a journal exercise or a call to action. I also created **Soul Stems** which are explained below. I also created a **Hint.**

In each chapter, there is a meditation that will allow you to use your visualization skills to manifest as well as to quiet your mind. You will develop a relationship with your inner "**Self**" and have a sense of coming home to "**Your-Self**." If you want a **deeper, more personalized experience** of this book's message, go to candesscampbell.com and click **Self-Help Tools**. You'll find more resources there.

Dr. Campbell is currently providing private psychic medium readings through video, phone, email, and in person. She also has public events. Schedule a session by purchasing a session at candesscampbell.com

Soul Stems

In this book, we will be using Soul Stems. A Soul Stem is a writing prompt that directs your writing and opens you up to your intuitive self. There are two ways to use a Soul Stem. One is to just finish the sentence. There may be several sentences, and doing this quickly without thinking can provide you with surprising information. You can also take your journal and complete the sentence, writing for 10 – 20 minutes. At first, you may be resistant, but stay with the process— it works!

When working with a Soul Stem, rather than writing from your head, you tap into your subconscious and you may bring up parts of **yourSelf** you have not consciously encountered before. You are so much more than your conscious mind, and when you have access to your whole **Being,** you are vaster than you can imagine. You may want to have a fast writing pen so you can write quickly and not think too much. Just let your stream of thoughts go onto the page. You may prefer to type depending on which works best for you. I suggest you use both of these tools in your process. I welcome testimonials of the experiences you have using the **Soul Stem** journaling process. It's amazing!

Meditation

During the meditations in this book, you will be asked to visualize something. Prior to the meditation, use the following exercise to prepare yourSelf.

In the **Self-Help Toolbox** at candesscampbell.com, there is information about "**Grounding** and other tools." On the website, there is also a 12 Minute Energy Meditation that helps you to center, ground, and run your energy, clearing stress and other people's energy from your energy field.

Sit in an upright position with your spine straight. Take a couple of deep breaths. Relax your body. Allow yourSelf to relax into your sitting position. Listen to the sounds that are close by and then listen to the sounds far away. Focus on your breath for a few minutes and just relax. Bring your attention to between your eyes and a little above your eyes. Now, bring your attention to the center of your head— this is your third eye. Envision a blue triangle that you look through with a gaze. Soften your eyes. When thoughts come up, just let them go by.

You can continue to breathe and focus far away through this triangle with softened eyes or you can now do the visualization exercise in each chapter. This meditation will help you to clear your mind.

Message to the Universe

"Ask and it shall be given" is true for many who understand the process of prayer and manifesting. What you focus upon increases, and what you let go of with expectancy can come back in a more magnificent way than you can imagine. Several years ago, when I was thinking of expanding my business, I was thinking of some spiritual leaders whose books I own. I asked myself, "What are they doing that I'm not doing?" I thought, well, they have published books and they also have people to promote them. I asked the Universe (saying to the Creator, the Divine), "I would like someone to promote me." Then, I set out to write my book *12 Weeks to Self-Healing: Transforming Pain through Energy Medicine.*

Sometimes later, a man from Japan contacted me through my website to receive a **DNA Activation**. I provided the service to him. Next, he contacted me and wanted me to do a psychic reading with him. He sent me his questions and I completed the reading and emailed it to him. He responded by saying he wanted to visit me. I was delighted and offered for him to stay with me. I picked him up from the airport and showed him his room. I continued with my day of working with clients. After work, we talked for a while and then a sense came over me. I shared with him, "Hiro, I had asked the Universe for someone to promote me. Is that you?"

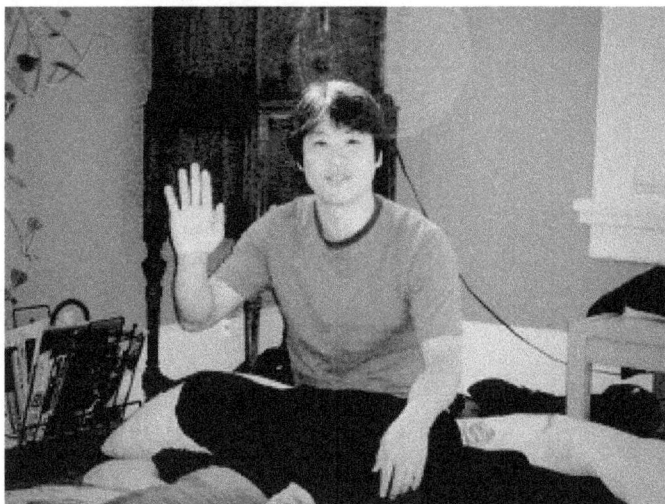

"Yes!" he responded. This process of connecting with Hiro took about a year. Not long after that, we created a working relationship that has been abundant in so many ways. We created a beautiful friendship that has served us for over 10 years now. As this book is being published we are working on a new Japanese website to better provide services to the Japanese clients.

After reading each chapter, you can create a message to the Universe. Just like my creation, ask for what you want to manifest. Know that you have a Higher Self, Essence Self, a Goddess/God Self and God/Goddess to assist you in your creations. That is not even counting the Angels and Guides. Become clear on what you desire. Feel what you would feel living that manifestation. Allow the Universe to re-create itself in order to assist you.

Enjoy the journey!

Chapter One

Everyone Has 24 Hours in a Day

*Happiness is when what you think, what you say,
and what you do are in harmony.*

— **Mahatma Gandhi**

Have you felt like you had to juggle it all to make your commitments each day? Whether you're scattered or organized, most of us tend to over-schedule ourselves. Even the weekends get planned so tightly that by Monday, you feel tired and ready for a break. Do you have trouble distinguishing between what is important and what becomes a habit?

I remember one day when my daughter Charisma was young, she asked me to take her to go play with a friend. My response was that I was too busy and couldn't take her — I didn't have time. She looked at me and said, "Mom, everyone has 24 hours in a day." Interestingly, this statement shocked me! I didn't realize I had wound myself so tight; I wasn't even aware of how much I had over-scheduled and

how it affected my children. We all have 24- hours a day! You can choose how you spend your time.

Several years ago, in an intuitive session with a client, I saw an image of an open book in his heart chakra. In this book, I saw several countries and several cultures. When I shared this, he said that he and his wife had planned to travel when they retired, but she had become ill with cancer. He said that she wanted him to do some traveling without her. I sensed he was grieving and didn't want to go alone. From the image in his heart, though, I sensed that if he didn't go, he would suffer energetically, having dreamed of his trip for years. Energy stuck in the heart chakra, or any chakra can create stress and possibly illness. If his wife felt guilty because he didn't go, like he suggested, this may affect her health negatively as well. His choices were many. I am not sure what he decided to do, but my hope is that he was able to travel with a friend or children and record the trip and share it with his wife. As a friend of mine always says, "Life is short."

Opportunity

Soul stems

What takes up too much of my time is . . .

What I really want to do is . . .

If I were living my dream life today and had all the resources (time, money, support), I would be . . .

I am energized when . . .

I am exhausted when . . .

One small step I can make today to free up time is . . .

Hint

It takes less time and energy to plan and execute something fun than it does to keep rehashing reasons why you should not do it!

Meditation

Sit in an upright position with your spine straight. Take a couple of deep breaths. Relax your body. Allow yourSelf to relax into your sitting position. Listen to the sounds that are close by and then listen to the sounds far away. Focus on your breath for a few minutes and just relax. Bring your attention between your eyes and a little above your eyes— this is your third eye. Envision a blue triangle that you look through with a gaze. Soften your eyes— when thoughts come up, just let them go by.

Look over the answers to your **Soul Stem** exercise. Write out what you want to create. As you create in your life what you desire, time expands, and the energy that has been focused on what you do not want will shift. Visualize yourSelf living your dream. See yourSelf relaxing and enjoying what you desire. Use your senses to really experience what you desire. Feel it, sense it, and live it in the visualization now.

Message to the Universe

After you have created the image of what you desire, send the message to the Universe. Let it go and don't take it back. Let it be and know it will unfold. Be sure to be open to it unfolding differently than you might expect.

Some people like to create a God/Goddess Box. This is any box you like, be it simple or ornate. Write out your desire and give it to God/Goddess/Universe by placing your intension in the box and leaving it. Check back in a few weeks or months and you will be surprised how well you manifest!

Chapter Two

Your Amazing Senses and Stress

If you look the right way, you can see that the whole world is a garden.

— **Frances Hodgson Burnett, the Secret Garden**

You may not be aware of how much sensory input you receive all day long. Your senses pick up millions of pieces of information all at once and translate this information into something you understand. Can you image this process!

Rather than seeing objects themselves, this is how it works:

1. Your eyes take in light waves that reflect off surfaces. These waves of light are then converted into neural impulses. Your brain then receives these neurological signals for interpretation.

2. Your ears pick up vibrations that travel to receptor cells, sending messages to the brain. Your brain then uses memory to help translate the messages.

3. Your sense of taste is created when your saliva dissolves chemical substances. Your taste buds interpret the sensations of sweet, sour, salty, bitter, and umami.

4. Your sense of smell is created by chemical molecules that you breathe in, and the messages are sent to the olfactory bulb at the base of the brain.

5. On your skin, there are millions of sensory receptors that trigger nerve impulses that communicate with the somatosensory cortex of the brain. Neurotransmitters (Brain chemicals) are then released into your body, which gives you the sensation of feeling. All this sensory input creates stress!

Your body responds to stress by activating the nervous system and releasing hormones. The adrenal glands respond and produce adrenaline and cortisol, releasing them into the bloodstream. This, in turn, causes your heart rate to rise and increases your breathing rate, and blood pressure. The blood flow increases in your muscles and your body stands **on alert**. Your pupils dilate, and glucose is released to increase your energy. **Your body is ready to respond quickly.** Bodies are incredible this way.

What happens when you experience continued stress? Your body doesn't return to the natural rest state. It continues on alert, producing low levels of stress hormones.

Over a period of time, because your body doesn't reset itself, your adrenals become fatigued and leave you feeling overwhelmed and depleted. Your body's immune system becomes compromised and this may create illness.

Humans are not the only ones negatively affected by the environment. Leatherback turtles are at risk of becoming extinct. The females lay their eggs and immediately return to the sea. Artificial light gets in the way of the females and their babies' ability to find the sea by the moon's light. They get lost and die from exhaustion and dehydration.

With continual stimulus, no wonder you become overwhelmed, stressed, and reactive rather than feeling calm and peaceful! Think about your own environment: your home, your work area, neighborhood, city, and where you go for entertainment. Do you provide yourSelf with enough quiet and peaceful time to integrate all the information you access every day?

Opportunity

Take time to look at your home and see if you have a calm, relaxed place where you can take 5 – 10 minutes to sit, breathe, and rest a couple of times per day.

Think about your **work area**. Can you relax there? Is it noisy? Are the floors or walls concrete? Do you have sunlight? Do you sit or stand all day? Do the colors soothe or energize you?

How about your **neighborhood**? Do you have a place where you can go to sit and relax, such as a park or a quiet neighborhood café? Are your neighbors quiet or noisy? Is there a lot of traffic, or are you on a peaceful country road?

What do you do for **fun**?

Do you keep yourSelf so **active** that you cannot integrate all the information you take in? Do you keep going because you are afraid you will miss something? Do you stay so busy so you don't feel your feelings? Do you get out and get the fresh air and healthy stimulation you need?

Use your journal to write out what you noticed about your own environment; what stresses you and how you find p eaceful a nd c alm r elaxation. L ist t he c hanges you need to make in your environment to bring rest and peace to your life.

Commit yourSelf to increase the time you spend resting in a peaceful environment. Choose to take 5 - 10 minutes three times per day to pull away from your busy lifestyle and just rest within.

You will find complimentary audios at candesscampbell. com under the Self-Help Tab. One audio will guide you into trance and the other will take you into a deep, relaxed state in order to replenish you after a busy day.

Using Essential Oils for stress and healing is not only amazing, but they are also fun to use. Not all essential oils are of the same quality. You may want to talk with friends to see what they use or do some research. In my office, I have a blend of Young Living Valor for grounding, Pan-Away for pain and clarity to support thinking. Bach Flower Essences are also a great choice.

Hint

To pre-pave the experience, use an essential oil, such as laven- der **when you are already deeply relaxed**. *Put some on your wrist and right under your nose. Later, when you are stressed and ready to rest, use the lavender to transport you more quickly into a resting state.*

Meditation

Sit in an upright position with your spine straight. Take a couple of deep breaths. Relax your body. Allow yourSelf to relax into your sitting position. Listen to the sounds that are close by and then listen to the sounds far away. Focus on your breath for a few minutes and just relax. Bring your attention between your eyes and a little above your eyes — this is your third eye. Envision a blue triangle that you look through with a gaze. Soften your eyes. When thoughts come up, just let them go by.

Notice how your body feels. Scan your body from the top of your head down to the tips of your toes. Move slowly as you notice what is going on in your body. Allow your body to move in whatever way it needs to achieve greater comfort.

Focus in your heart. Imagine your heart as a loving and safe environment. Image someone you love and feel them in your heart. Scan your body again and notice how your body feels when you are focused on your heart. Use this meditation as often as you like when you take time to rest for 5 – 10 minutes per day.

Message to the Universe

Once you have practiced being relaxed, send a message to the Universe of gratitude and appreciation for how wonderful it feels to be in a relaxed, healing environment. Feel the joy well up in your heart. Allow this joy and gratitude to support you all day long!

Chapter Three

Evaluating Stressors in Your Life

I was a little excited but mostly blorft. "Blorft" is an adjective I just made up that means 'Completely overwhelmed, but proceeding as if everything is fine and reacting to the stress with the torpor of a possum.' I have been blorft every day for the past seven years.

— Tina Fey, Bossypants

Now, let's look at some of the stressors in your life. First, look over the Stress Symptoms at the end of this book. You can also assess yourSelf from the Life Events Stress Test in the **Self-Help Toolbox**. Take the Holmes and Rahe Stress Scale. This will give you a good indication of your risk for illness based on situations you have experienced in the last year of your life.

It is time to reduce the stress. Let's determine your pattern. Are you Hurried and Harried and always busy, planning, organizing, attending, re-organizing, driving, and volunteering, and then at the end of the day, you can't shut down your mind?

Or are you Paralyzed and Pallid with a lot to do. Do you get so overwhelmed that you keep putting things off? Do you hide, wait or procrastinate until you can barely function? Both of these responses to stress may have to do with having too much to do.

Do you respond daily to an ongoing list of "Shoulds?" Are you on automatic pilot and walking through the day without much thought of the decisions you make?

One way to become too busy is to get in the habit of saying yes. If you thought about it, would you say no? Many of us were not taught to set boundaries and don't have an understanding of boundaries at all. Let's explore the internal and external boundaries. Internal boundaries have to do with setting self-boundaries and external boundaries are set regarding others.

Examples of **internal boundaries** might be:

1. Stopping to rest when you are tired.

2. Rather than repeating yourSelf over and over again to get someone to behave differently, you change your own behavior.

3. Speaking appropriately when you want to be heard rather than spurting out words and regretting what you said.

4. Taking time to nurture yourSelf, so you renew and regenerate.

Examples of **external boundaries** might be:

1. Saying yes, when you mean yes and saying no when you mean no.
2. Walking away from abuse or disrespect.
3. Setting a limit and walking away when someone is not respectful of your time.
4. Expecting shared responsibility in a relationship and setting guidelines.

Opportunity

Take a moment to think about what you did yesterday. How much of what you did was what you really wanted to do? What behaviors were habits or "Shoulds?" If you were not on automatic pilot, what would you have done differently? Write this out in your journal.

Identify your pattern. **Is your tendency to be hurried or paralyzed?**

If you are **hurried**, write out all the things you have to do that are undone. Now, go through them and give three stars (***) to the items that you absolutely have to accomplish. Write the date you will have them completed. The items that can be done but are not necessary at this time, give two stars (**). For items that really don't have to be done or will just get done in the process of your daily life, draw a line through them or delete them. Is this more manageable?

If your tendency is to be **paralyzed**, write out a list of what it is you are avoiding. Choose one task a day to focus upon. With fifteen minutes a day of focused attention, you can lighten your load! You can also use these Soul Stems to assist you in becoming more aware of what stresses you. Your inner guide will show you how to lessen your stress.

If this were done, I would . . .

The reason I can't do this is . . .

I am afraid when . . .

I trust myself most when . . .

I am most supported by . . .

Be gentle with yourSelf and don't overload yourSelf. You may want to choose one timed writing a day and then reflect upon it.

You will find valuable information in the Self-Help Toolbox at candesscampbell.com. Enjoy releasing stress, self-assessments about boundaries and audio lessons to assist you in becoming clear on creating healthy choices.

Hint

Although, you may be afraid to set boundaries for fear of others being angry or leaving you, what actually happens is they respect you more. If someone leaves because you set a healthy boundary . . . Well, enough said.

Meditation

Sit in an upright position with your spine straight. Take a couple of deep breaths. Relax your body. Allow yourSelf to relax into your sitting position. Listen to the sounds that are close by and then listen to the sounds far away. Focus on your breath for a few minutes and just relax. Bring your attention between your eyes and a little above your eyes— this is your third eye. Envision a blue triangle that you look through with a gaze. Soften your eyes. When thoughts come up, just let them go by.

Image yourSelf alone, feeling a golden, white light around you, swirling from your heart throughout your body and surrounding you in a sense of relaxed, calm bliss. Now, imagine people you are close to, family or friends, coming into the space around you one at a time. Notice how you feel when each person is in your energy field. Just relax and notice. When you are done, make some notes in your journal.

Message to the Universe

See yourSelf surrounded by those you love in a healthy way. Let the Universe know that you are open to receiving love and support from those who can offer this to you in a healthy way. Open yourSelf up to receive healthy support from the Universe and from those you love.

Chapter Four

The Speed of Your Mind

*If a cluttered desk is a sign of a cluttered mind, of
what, then, is an empty desk a sign?*

— Laurence J. Peter

After a day at work, do you find your mind racing? Do you have trouble sleeping at night? Do you lie there as you try to fall asleep or wake up in the middle of the night and ruminate? This is where **Live Simply: Less is More** will assist you in clearing your mind.

One way to empty your mind is to journal. I have been journaling for over forty years, and it has helped get rid of the "chatter" and deepen my relationship with my Self. If you would prefer to journal on paper, I suggest an inexpensive spiral notebook so you can get messy on the page. This is a process of emptying your mind.

The Soul Stem writing process is called automatic or stream-of-consciousness writing. You put your pen to paper, preferably with a fast-writing pen, and write whatever comes to your mind. Start with a simple sentence, such as "If I were to travel anywhere . . ." Just follow your thought processes and keep writing. If you find you are resistant, just write what comes to your mind. Don't stop and don't lift your pen! Continue, even if you are writing, "I don't know what to write— I don't know what to write." Continue until something else surfaces.

You can find more about the Soul Stem process in the Self-Help Toolbox at candesscampbell.com. You may also be interested in my previous book on journaling **Live Intuitively: Journal the Wisdom of your Soul.**

Another way to quiet your mind is meditation. In addition to what you have been practicing, there are several other ways to meditate, and two simple methods are outlined in the paragraphs below.

One way to practice meditation is to focus on your breathing. Gently focus on your breath. Your mind may wander, but allow thoughts to just go by and don't attach to them. Don't push them away or pull them towards you. Just let your thoughts go by and continue to focus on your breathing. Sometimes, people get confused when attempting meditation and give up because they can't make their thoughts go away. You have a central nervous system and will always have thoughts or sensations. Just experience them and let them go by. I found that meditating first thing in the morning before getting out of bed works best. Your mind is still in a trance state from sleep, and you haven't yet filled it with daily activities.

Another way to meditate is with sound. The sound that I like is in three parts. Begin with "Ah,"...add "oh oh,"...and finish with "mmm." Ah – oh - mmm. Begin by doing this out loud and then do it silently within.

This is your meditation process. Try the two methods, see what you like and then practice daily. Don't give up if you don't get the results you want immediately. It takes time. If you have a harder time letting go of your thoughts, remember there is a grounding and centering meditation audio on my site that will guide you. You can follow this meditation with your mind. It is one of my favorites, and I use it often.

Opportunity

Take a moment to write your sleeping pattern in your journal.

1. What time do you go to bed?
2. What do you do for three hours prior to bed?
3. When in bed do you read, watch TV, listen to a podcast or go right to sleep?
4. Do you use sleeping aids, such as a prescription medication or an OTC medicine?
5. How long does it take for you to fall asleep?
6. Do you sleep through the night? If not, what do you think about when you wake? What do you do when you wake?

It is helpful to do the following three hours before going to bed:

1. Avoid eating and exercising.
2. Avoid stimulating television, radio shows, podcasts or online shows.
3. Have a hot cup of chamomile or nettle tea to relax you.

Here are some **Soul Stems** to use to help clear your mind. I suggest you do these as a daily practice. You can also use them when you wake in the middle of the night. There are also Soul Stems to balance your life at candesscampbell.com.

What excites me the most is . . .

What bothers me the most is . . .

I can't wait until I . . .

If only I would have . . .

If I had more time, I would . . .

If I had more rest, I would . . .

Put a time in your calendar to meditate. Set your timer for 15 minutes. Understand that when beginning to meditate, you may not be able to become clear and restful. Be gentle with yourSelf, but continue daily until you feel comfortable with your process.

Reward yourSelf as being successful when you sit for the 15 minutes and not by what happened during the meditation. Your experience will change and you will become comfortable.

Hint

Journaling and Meditating in the morning are easiest. You have just awakened and you have access to images and senses from your dreams, which I believe is your Higher-Self communicating with you.

Meditation

Sit in an upright position with your spine straight. Take a couple of deep breaths. Relax your body. Allow yourSelf to relax into your sitting position. Listen to the sounds that are close by and then listen to the sounds far away. Focus on your breath for a few minutes and just relax. Bring your attention to between your eyes and a little above your eyes— this is your third eye. Envision a blue triangle that you look through with a gaze. Soften your eyes. When thoughts come up, just let them go by.

Look over the answers to your Soul Stem exercise. Write out what you want to create. As you create in your life what you desire, time expands, and the energy that has been focused on what you do not want will shift. Visualize yourSelf living your dream. See yourSelf relaxing and enjoying what you desire. Use your senses to really experience what you desire. Feel it, sense it and live it in the visualization now.

Message to the Universe

Now that you are tuning into your body, the message to the Universe today may be what you received during your meditation. Whether you realized you are too serious, or found your body was achier than you thought, it may be a wake up call for you. You may have received a message to call a friend or to change your career. Just listen and more will be revealed. When you sit in meditation first create an intention like peace, love, or courage. Listen and allow your feelings of love to guide you.

Chapter Five

Living in the Margins

I believe in moderation.
But I wouldn't overdo it.

— **Joseph Ferguson, Southbound**

few months ago, it became apparent to me that I was writing in the margins. I noticed when I was typing that I changed the paper margins to get more information on the page until the margins became almost non-existent. At that moment, all of a sudden I realized that this was also how I had been living my life! I was living in the margins. I put so much in a day that I had no margin left. If there was a last-minute concert or movie, I couldn't go. There was no margin to expand, no room for spontaneity.

Back in the day when I used a paper calendar, I color-fully scheduled in "Shapeless time." Shapeless time was for whatever I wanted, whether it was to finish a project, read a book or take a walk. It didn't matter what it was;

it was **my** time. Without noticing, I fell out of the habit of scheduling time for myself.

How do you integrate time for yourSelf?

Opportunity

In your journal, write for 10 - 20 minutes and complete each of the following Soul Stems:

If I had more time . . .

I have a lot of fun when I . . .

When I am alone . . .

What I love about having free time is . . .

When I spend time resting, I . . .

I am most creative when . . .

Happiness comes from . . .

What I love about my life is . . .

See what comes up for you. You will find more exercises and information at candesscampbell.com. Next, look at your upcoming week and the month and create shapeless time.

Hint

Although you may think it is because of this person or that situation, whether or not you take time for yourSelf is absolutely up to you. The more you increase the time you spend doing what you really love and want to do, the stressors that hack into your precious time will begin to retreat!

Meditation

Sit in an upright position with your spine straight. Take a couple of deep breaths. Relax your body. Allow yourSelf to relax into your sitting position. Listen to the sounds that are close by and then listen to the sounds far away. Focus on your breath for a few minutes and just relax. Bring your attention to between your eyes and a little above your eyes— this is your third eye. Envision a blue triangle that you look through with a gaze. Soften your eyes. When thoughts come up, just let them go by.

Look over the answers to your Soul Stem exercise. Write out what you want to create. As you create in your life what you desire, time expands, and the energy that has been focused on what you do not want will shift. Visualize yourSelf living your dream. See yourSelf relaxing and enjoying what you desire. Use your senses to really experience what you desire. Feel it, sense it, and live it in the visualization now.

Message to the Universe

This is a message I know well and not because I give in easily! Your heart message to the Universe today is "I surrender!"

Chapter Six

Quieting Down

*There comes a time when the world gets quiet and
the only thing left is your own heart. So you'd better
learn the sound of it. Otherwise, you'll never
understand what its saying.*

— Sarah Dessen, Just Listen

Have you ever noticed what you do when you get home from work? Do you go to the fridge to find something sweet or salty? Do you eat or drink something caffeinated? Do you reach for a spritzer or a glass of wine? Do you sit in front of the TV and watch the news, a sitcom or a reality show before dinner? How do you transition from your workday to your private time when you get home?

Many people have a difficult time slowing down and quieting down. They go from a busy workday world to a home where they distract themselves with more stimulation.

What would happen if you walked in the door, poured yourSelf a glass of pure water (Many of us are dehydrated), and sat and closed your eyes and just breathed for 15 minutes? This is not even about meditation, although meditation can restore and balance you. It is about resting and breathing. The transition from work to home is often a difficult one. Using sugary or salty foods or caffeinated or alcoholic drinks are often how people push through and keep doing more.

When you are out of balance after working all day without rest, your body wants to resume balance. The Chinese have the concept of Yin and Yang. Yin is expansive, and Yang is contracted. After working all day, you may feel extremely contracted and want to expand. Alcohol and sugary foods are expanding, so you reach for something to eat or drink that will expand you. Being on the computer is expansive, so when you get home, you may want something to help you contract.

The **Self-Help Toolbox** provides information about the Yin and Yang properties of food and activities. Here, we will explore a couple of ideas.

When you need to relax after an intense, busy day and are contracted and need to become more Yin, rather than reaching for an alcoholic drink, you may want to have a piece of fruit, a fruit salad or a smoothie. According to Cheyenne Mendel, an acupuncturist and Bazi practitioner trained in Chinese medicine, "Many times, people reach for something to put in their bodies when, in fact, they are just chronically dehydrated. Your insides are contracted like shrink wrap, so the hunger kicks in when there is a need for water." Another suggestion is to go for a gentle stroll for 10 to 20 minutes. You can also just lie on your bed, the floor or a yoga mat and allow your body to be supported and breathe for 15 minutes.

Here are a few ways to pull yourSelf back from the world when you are too expanded, too spacey, and too Yin. My 'go-to' is to pick up my journal and just start writing. Another way is to have a cup of miso soup, some root vegetables or protein such as chicken, fish or nuts. Rubbing your feet, doing some yoga or reading would be helpful as well. Having someone rub your feet, of course, is the best!

Opportunity

1. Practice sitting and just breathing as soon as you get home from work once per day for the next three days. Once you realize how good it feels to just breathe, commit to doing this for a month. Put up a reminder on your mirror or schedule it in your phone calendar.

2. Take a few minutes each day while at work to sit, close your eyes and focus on your breath. Doing this for 3 - 5 minutes a couple of times per day can make a big difference.

3. Keep healthy snacks with you for your travel home. This simple idea can help the transition from work to home and balance your blood sugar.

4. Take time to retreat from the busyness of your home for a few minutes and read or listen to music. Even if you live alone, having a special retreat place is helpful to reconnect with yourSelf. If you don't yet have this kind of place, creating it is fun and rewarding.

Hint

Many are afraid to quiet their minds for fear of what may surface. What happens often is your critical self shows up first. As soon as this happens, call in the part of you that is loving and nurturing. If you have not made a connection with this part of you, use your journal and write a letter to yourSelf of commitment to being compassionate, loving and gentle with yourSelf.

Meditation

Sit in an upright position with your spine straight. Take a couple of deep breaths. Relax your body. Allow yourSelf to relax into your sitting position. Listen to the sounds that are close by and then listen to the sounds far away. Focus on your breath for a few minutes and just relax. Bring your attention to between your eyes and a little above your eyes. This is your third eye. Envision a blue triangle that you look through with a gaze. Soften your eyes. When thoughts come up, just let them go by.

Look over the answers to your Soul Stem exercise. Write out what you want to create. As you create in your life what you desire, time expands, and the energy that has been focused on what you do not want will shift. Visualize yourSelf living your dream. See yourSelf relaxing and enjoying what you desire. Use your senses to really experience what you desire. Feel it, sense it, and live it in the visualization now.

Message to the Universe

Sit quietly and feel the love in your heart and silently let the Universe know you are ready to receive!

Chapter Seven

Numbing Out

*If he were any other man, I might have suspected him
of substance abuse, of being cooked up or something.
But Barrons was too much a purist for that; his
drugs were money, power, and control.*

— Karen Marie Moning, Darkfever

When your life gets too busy and you become overwhelmed, you may unconsciously find ways to numb
yourSelf. When stress builds and you haven't found effective ways to manage your stress, you may start using substances. Alcohol and other drugs, such as cannabis and
sedatives, may seem helpful initially, but the relaxation or
high you get can result in creating more stress. When using
these substances to relax, you may begin to have difficulty
focusing and staying on task. You can also develop a toler-
ance to the drug. This means that you need more of the substance to obtain the same relaxation or high you received
previously. With substance abuse and addiction, there is

also a denial factor. You may not be able to see that alcohol and/or other drug use has become a problem. You may be at risk of becoming dependent and becoming addicted. If someone who knows you well tells you that you have a problem with a substance or addictive behavior, believe them! I'm a strong advocate of both 12 Step Programs and Refuge Recovery groups.

Other than substances, there are Process Addictions as well. Some of the more common process addictions are gambling, shopping, workaholism, and more recently, Internet gaming. With easy access to pornography on smartphones, sex addiction has become more common as well. These behaviors begin as a way to gently numb or distract you. You can use them to relieve your stress, but eventually, they may create more problems. For some, the numbing becomes a distraction that gets out of control. At that point, you start seeing the negative results. More likely a loved one will tell you they think you have a problem. This is where counseling or treatment is needed.

Opportunity

In the Self-Help Toolbox, you will find a substance abuse self-assessment and an assessment for the process of addiction. There are also solutions to reduce or eliminate the use of these substances and the processes of addiction.

In your journal, use the Soul Stem Process to answer these questions as honestly as you can in your 10 - 20 minute timed writing.

What stresses me the most is . . .

When I am stressed I . . .

The best way for me to rest is . . .

The substances I use to relax or unwind are . . . (Alcohol, cannabis, Rx meds, food, etc.)

My gut tells me I need to cut down on or stop using . . .

The process addictions that alarm me are . . . (Workaholism, Gaming, Gambling, etc.)

The people who are concerned about my use and my health are . . .

The best way for me to rest and unwind is to . . .

The commitment I make to myself today is . . .

Some resources you can use to find balance are meditation classes, yoga, exercise, support groups online or in-person and 12 Step and Refuge Recovery Meetings.

Hint

We cannot heal and grow on our own. As much as we may resist it, we need each other!

Meditation

Sit in an upright position with your spine straight. Take a couple of deep breaths. Relax your body. Allow yourSelf to relax into your sitting position. Listen to the sounds that are close by and then listen to the sounds far away. Focus on your breath for a few minutes and just relax. Bring your attention to between your eyes and a little above your eyes— this is your third eye. Envision a blue triangle that you look through with a gaze. Soften your eyes. When thoughts come up, just let them go by.

Look over the answers to your Soul Stem exercise. Write out what you want to create. As you create in your life what you desire, time expands, and the energy that has been focused on what you do not want will shift. Visualize yourSelf living your dream. See yourSelf relaxing and enjoying what you desire. Use your senses to really experience what you desire. Feel it, sense it, and live it in the visualization now.

Message to the Universe

Today, the message to the universe is physical. Take some time to sit outside and just appreciate what you see. Take a walk and just receive the sounds of nature— the Universe hears you loud and clear.

Chapter Eight

Clearing Your Space and Mind

At some point I realized that I wasn't organizing my life; I was organizing my clutter.

— **Francine Jay**

Have you ever noticed that after clearing off your desk or cleaning out your purse or briefcase, you feel a lot more organized? Do you notice that you think more clearly? Your inner mind indeed reflects your outer environment, and your external environment affects your mind. Feng Shui experts teach about the flow of energy and how the placement of objects can affect your life and your health. The chi, or life force, gets stuck, and it can create an imbalance or even illness.

Several years ago, my former husband and I were looking for a home to buy. Our vision was a country home near a source of water. One home we looked at was sitting in a narrow valley between two mountains nearby. When I looked at the placement of the house, I thought energy would get stuck between the two mountains and whoever lived in that house would most likely get sick. I asked the realtor why the couple was selling. He shared with us that both people who lived there were ill and had to move closer to their children. Energy must be able to flow and not become stagnant. Sometimes, clutter can stop the movement of energy as well.

Have you ever found out that you bought two or more of the same book, forgetting you already bought it, yet never read it? Do you have several of the same items or many items that you don't use? Does the clutter make it difficult to find anything? How about technology? Do you know how to use all the features of your camera, phone and computer? Are you so overwhelmed with the electronic toys that you can't remember how to use them? Maybe you can't even find them!

The concept of "Less is more" does not only mean having less clutter and using what you have but also learning to live within your means! When you make purchases, focus on quality, not quantity. Use what you have before you buy something new.

Now is the time to make the commitment to clear your space. Notice what you use easily, without effort and regularly. A good rule of thumb is if you don't use it or love it, give it away or sell it. You can begin by going through your home, room-by-room, and finding one item that you really don't use or need each day. Create two piles, one "Give away" pile and one "Sell" pile. If the object is not worth much, you can save money and time by just giving it away to charity. You can even write the donation amount off on your taxes.

Opportunity

1. Stop right now and set your timer or watch for 15 minutes. Pick an area of your house that needs some organization. Choose a drawer, bookshelf or even the kitchen table. Choose something that is manageable in a short amount of time. Organize and come back.

   That felt great, didn't it? When you take 15 or 20-minute time intervals, it makes organizing manageable, and the reward is great. Another way to organize if you watch TV is to get up and organize during commercials!

2. Sit and visualize your home. List in your journal the areas you need to clear out. Assign an order to the list and commit to begin the clearing. Start with small areas, so you feel successful. Next, pick an area where you feel the most overwhelmed by clutter. Break it down into smaller areas. It can be helpful to have paper bags or plastic containers to put items in that will take longer, such as paperwork or items you might find in a junk drawer. Clear the area, using one bag or container at a time, and either put the things away, give them away or add them to the "sale" pile.

I watched my daughter do this and it was a great idea. When organizing paperwork, you can bring the bag into the living room and go through it when you are watching TV, listening to music or at the kitchen table when you are talking with your loved ones.

3. If the idea of touching the mess or moving anything is too much for you, take your journal and use these Soul Stems:

I am most overwhelmed when . . .

I feel secure when . . .

If I was organized, I'd be . . .

A simple step I can make today is . . .

4. Call a friend or a family member who can come over and be with you when you organize. This shared energy, even if they don't help, makes the task seem easier.

5. Set up a family or neighborhood yard sale. As you do this, you will find it easier and easier to let go of items you don't use. Allow someone to be your muse for the organization.

And last, and maybe the best for you, hire a home organizer or even a housekeeper to help you begin this process. It will be well worth the money spent. Since the last edit of this book, I have learned about Marie Kondo and the KonMari method of tidying up that brings you Joy! She will help you organize. She has a Netflix show called Tidying Up. I highly recommend it.

Hint

The trunk of my car is my giveaway pile. You may want to use your trunk or a container in your trunk to store give-away items. Choose a charity near where you normally drive and when you are out running errands you can drop off the items. They will give you a receipt for your taxes too! You may also have a charity that regularly picks up items from your home. A quick phone call to set this up may be a great motivation to get started clearing!

Meditation

Sit in an upright position with your spine straight. Take a couple of deep breaths. Relax your body. Allow yourSelf to relax into your sitting position. Listen to the sounds that are close by and then listen to the sounds far away. Focus on your breath for a few minutes and just relax. Bring your attention to between your eyes and a little above your eyes— this is your third eye. Envision a blue triangle that you look through with a gaze. Soften your eyes. When thoughts come up, just let them go by.

Look over the answers to your Soul Stem exercise. Write out what you want to create. As you create in your life what you desire, time expands, and the energy that has been focused on what you do not want will shift. Visualize yourSelf living your dream. See yourSelf relaxing and enjoying what you desire. Use your senses to really experience what you desire. Feel it, sense it and live it in the visualization now.

Message to the Universe

Contemplate how you can help reduce toxins on the planet. Make a commitment to make one change and validate yourSelf for this choice.

Chapter Nine

Joy from Receiving!

*Allow yourSelf to receive. It's your right and respon-
sibility to care for yourself and then others.*

— Candess M. Campbell

Today, many people want to create less in their lives.
They are exhausted from doing and giving too much.
Often, they are the ones who volunteer, raise their hands,
step up and help. They buy things and do for others, but
not for themselves, and on and on the cycle goes.

This is often an indication that they overdo and over-
give. It's time to allow yourSelf to receive and allow Joy
into your life. One way to allow yourSelf to receive is to
just stop saying yes. Compulsively saying yes becomes
an unconscious habit. Have you found that you say yes
without thinking and then resent the person to whom
you said yes? Do you neglect yourSelf or others while
following through on a commitment you wish you never
made?

I was with someone recently who offered to drive a great distance out of her way to be accommodating. I gave her every opportunity to choose differently, but I couldn't help taking the ride because I was so curious about how she was behaving. I took the ride. She was clearly angry that she was doing it, but rather than just say no, she suffered and everyone around her could feel the anger. I know that I said yes when I wanted to say no in the past, and it was sad to watch her so disconnected from her own truth.

One way you may avoid receiving is to always say no. Do friends or family offer to help you, and without even thinking, your automatic response is to say no? Sometimes, you may not want to accept help because you feel it's easier to do something yourSelf. This can be the case, but when you allow someone to help you, this forms a relationship that may be valuable to you now and in the future. You also learn to receive, and this allows others the joy of giving.

A simple way to become joyful through receiving is to allow time for yourSelf. We talked about shapeless time in a previous chapter, so I won't expand here. In addition to these suggestions, you can also treat yourSelf to something you really enjoy. What would you like? A day spent reading by yourSelf? A massage and spa treatment? A weekend playing golf? Taking the children to a relative's home for the night so you can have a break? Whatever it is that you truly desire, only you can make it happen.

Opportunity

1. In your journal, list the people with whom you continually say yes to when they ask. Then, complete the following Soul Stem for each person: "If I say no to _____, then . . ."

2. In your journal, list the people who have offered to help you. Write who you have allowed to help you and the result. Write who you have not allowed to help you when they offered and why.

3. Sometimes help comes from people you hire. You may allow yourSelf the help of a domestic worker, a lawn service, a tax accountant or financial planner. You may also choose a childcare worker, a personal shopper and having your car washed. List in your journal areas (in a perfect world) where you would like to have help. Then, choose one.

4. Many successful people have coaches. In our society, there is so much to do it's difficult to stay on track. Coaches can help. There are many types of coaching, such as financial coaches, exercise and health coaches, business coaches, motivational coaches, recovery coaches for addiction, relationship coaches, marketing coaches and many others. If you had time with a coach, what area would you choose? Write in your journal what you would like to accomplish. At **candesscampbell.com**, I have several questions listed that come from my coaching business. Answering these questions will guide you in the direction you want to go.

5. Do you really enjoy your life, or do you fill it with so much that you are always going from one task to the next?

Finish the following Soul Stems in your journal:

If I had a whole day to myself, I would. . .

If I had a week to relax, I would. . .

If I took an hour per day for myself, I would . . .

When I am elderly and looking back at my life, I will have wished I would have . . .

What I love about mySelf is . . .

Hint

Whether it's spring or winter, do you ever feel like you need some nature to calm or stimulate yourSelf?

Take a walk around the block or go to a local park. Maybe you need only go as far as your own yard. Cut off some branches with buds or flowers blooming and bring them indoors. Put the smaller branches in a small vase and the larger in a larger vase and infuse every room with the energy and wisdom of the plant, bush or tree. It is refreshing and you receive not only the beauty of nature, but the spirit of nature as well.

Meditation

Sit in an upright position with your spine straight. Take a couple of deep breaths. Relax your body. Allow yourSelf to relax into your sitting position. Listen to the sounds that are close by and then listen to the sounds far away. Focus on your breath for a few minutes and just relax. Bring your attention to between your eyes and a little above your eyes— this is your third eye. Envision a blue triangle that you look through with a gaze. Soften your eyes. When thoughts come up, just let them go.

Look over the answers to your Soul Stem exercise. Write out what you want to create. As you create in your life what you desire, time expands, and the energy that has been focused on what you do not want will shift. Visualize yourSelf living your dream. See yourSelf relaxing and enjoying what you desire. Use your senses to really experience what you desire. Feel it, sense it, and live it in the visualization now.

Message to the Universe

Once you experience nature and bring it indoors, sit and focus in your heart. Feel the love of nature and how it supports you. Receiving is a habit and once you learn to stop and listen and receive; you will be energized or relaxed from the release of stress. I live by the Spokane River and whether I am walking the river or just feeling the energy from my home, I am always receiving. Love to receive the sound of the birds in the morning, the Canadian geese flying overhead, and the rounded river rocks under my feet. Allow your senses to become saturated with the gifts of nature.

Chapter Ten

Rest

*A generous heart, kind speech, and a life of
service and compassion are the things which
renew humanity.*

— Buddha

Preventative rest has been forgotten in today's fast-paced
world. Do you find that you run yourSelf ragged and
rest only when you are ill or cannot go any longer?

The concept of **Live Simply: Less is More** came to me
soon after I completed my doctoral program in clinical
hypnotherapy. My dissertation became my first book, *12
Weeks to Self-Healing: Transforming Pain through Energy
Medicine.* My father died while I was in my doctoral program, and as part of my grieving, I was not able to read for
a year, so I took a leave of absence. The grief caused me to
read the same paragraph over and over, yet I was unable
to comprehend. When I decided to begin my doctoral program again, I had a deadline to meet. Either I finished the

coursework and write my dissertation, or I would lose all my credits. At the same time, I was traveling the world, facilitating workshops and seeing private clients.

I really wanted to just sit and be. I didn't want to do anything. I had pushed myself so hard that I was exhausted. I soon realized that I didn't want my life to be so full. I didn't want to hurry, I didn't want deadlines and I only wanted to live, to be fully alive and to rest!

I remember asking a friend if she wanted to go to downtown Spokane to see a movie. She looked at me and said, "No, I'm tired, and I need to go home and rest." This was an awakening for me! The lights came on! Prior to that, I had no concept of rest. Even though I had a successful practice as a mental health counselor, spiritual teacher, and intuitive reader and coach; caffeine and sugar pushed me through to the next project. I was driven to help others with a "save the world" complex. For years, I had been on automatic pilot.

What I understand now is that when you rest, you can actually create more. This happens in two ways that I am aware of, although I am sure there are more. When you rest, you naturally fall into a trance. A trance actually happens naturally every hour and a half or so. When you rest, you are able to access not only information from your conscious mind, but also from your subconscious and, I believe, your Higher Self. The other way that rest helps is that you learn to use a different part of yourSelf to manifest. Rather than making an effort to get something done, you manifest through envisioning what you are creating.

The Universe naturally flows into your life! When you allow the natural unfolding, you gain many opportunities that are missed when you are too busy. When you rest, you are able to notice what is right in front of you. You allow and receive the blessing of gifts from the Universe.

Writing *Live Simply: Less is More* has been a surprising gift for me. My gratitude continues to expand as I realize that this information came to me as a process of self-healing. I am blessed to be able to share this with you.

My hope is that *Live Simply: Less is More* will support you on your life journey, allowing you to create more shapeless time, increased self-awareness, less stress and to truly live in integrity with your desires.

Opportunity

1. Take time to journal several times each week. Check-in with yourSelf, enjoy a cup of tea, get comfortable and be restful as you journal. Allow this private time to help you to develop a relationship with your inner Self.

2. If you are in often in public and have to be "on," take time to pull in and nest. Say no to a party, activity or occasion. Let yourSelf stay home and do nothing. Yes, truly do nothing. Just sit and rest.

3. Find activities that are restful for you. Whether it is reading, playing Scrabble, ™ listening to music or watching TV, just rest.

4. Take a voice fast. My friend, Cheyenne, does this often. She will call me and tell me she is taking a voice fast for a day so that I know she will not be available. I love that she sets that boundary around herself and takes time to rest.

5. One of the most joyful ways for me to rest is to meditate. Find a practice or just sit and follow your breath. Set a timer for 20 minutes and just notice what happens. You cannot do it wrong. Just be.

Hint

Many people have a difficult time transitioning from a working state to a reset state. Begin by stopping once, then twice, and then three times a day to close your eyes and just breathe for 5 minutes. Feel your body. Feel your resistance. At first, it may be uncomfortable because you begin to think about or feel something uncomfortable. Just breathe and let it go and be present to yourSelf. Then when you transition from work time to rest time you will be able to take five minutes to move into rest. It supports your health more than unconsciously drinking a beer or wine or grabbing a bowl of ice cream or a bag of chips.

Meditation

Sit in an upright position with your spine straight. Take a couple of deep breaths. Relax your body. Allow yourSelf to relax into your sitting position. Listen to the sounds that are close by and then listen to the sounds far away. Focus on your breath for a few minutes and just relax. Bring your attention to between your eyes and a little above your eyes— this is your third eye. Envision a blue triangle that you look through with a gaze. Soften your eyes. When thoughts come up, just let them go.

Look over the answers to your Soul Stem exercise. Write out what you want to create. As you create in your life what you desire, time expands, and the energy that has been focused on what you do not want will shift. Visualize yourSelf living your dream. See yourSelf relaxing and enjoying what you desire. Use your senses to really experience what you desire. Feel it, sense it and live it in the visualization now.

Message to the Universe

To begin a process of meditation if you find the five-minute experience motivating, you can start with my 12 Minute Energy Clearing . If you prefer, you can just expand your five minutes up to ten and so forth. It helps to practice meditation when you first awake so that you don't have to clear all that has happened that day from your mind and you are already closely connected to your trance state.

For more tools, check out my **Self-Help Toolbox!**

List of Stress Symptoms

With your busy lifestyle, you may know you are stressed, but not be able to identify your stress symptoms. Here is a list you can work with.

Headaches

Poor Concentration

Forgetfulness

Difficulty making Decisions

Error in Judgment

Upset stomach

A knot in your stomach

Indigestion

Diarrhea

Overeating

Frequent Colds

Skipping Meals

Feeling uptight

Anxiety

Irritability

Anger

Clumsiness

Sense of Powerlessness

Lack of Hope

Lack of Energy

Oversleeping

Waking up in the night

Inability to fall asleep

Increased use of alcohol or other drugs

You will also find a Life Events Stress Scale in the Toolbox. If you find you have several of the symptoms, please contact your physician or health care provider to assist you further.

Acknowledgements

Immense gratitude goes to my friend, chosen sister, and Goddess extraordinaire, Cheyenne Mendel, for her help with the information about Yin and Yang. She has been a consistent, loving guidance in my life as well as a cornerstone of my personal health plan. She is an incredible acupuncturist, who is well studied in Chinese medicine and specializes in Bazi readings.

Referenced Sources and Resources

Holmes and Rahe Stress Scale
https://en.wikipedia.org/wiki/Holmes_and_Rahe_stress
_scale

Marie Kondo and the KonMari method.
https://konmari.com/

Here are some referenced tools from Candess M. Campbell.
Self-Help Toolbox
http://energymedicinedna.com/self-help-toolbox/

About the Author

Candess M. Campbell, PhD is a best-selling author, International Speaker, Psychic Medium, and Intuitive Consultant. Dr. Candess has been empowering and supporting others in healing for over 35 years. She graduated in 2009 with a Doctorate in Clinical Hypnotherapy from American Pacific University and in 1992 with a Master's in Counseling Psychology and in 1986 with a Bachelor's in Psychology and minor in Religious Studies from Gonzaga University.

Through her international travel connections and her presence online, Dr. Campbell assists others in healing themselves and healing the planet. She specializes in **DNA Activation** which raises your energetic vibration and Karmic Healing which is an Ascension Process. She tours the planet facilitating workshops, providing Psychic Readings and sharing her books.